*Printed in the United States of America
First Edition*

Cover Design by Michelle Muhammad

*Photo Credits
Marcel Jacobs*

Illustrations by Lakisha M. Tanksley

THERE IS AN OASIS

A Collection of
Motivational Poems by
Lakisha Marie Tanksley

A little about the author

LaKisha Marie Tanksley, a 22 year old Chicagoan, has earned an impressive reputation as an actress poet and motivational speaker. At the young age of 8, LaKisha began writing poetry. At the age of 14, she was nominated by the Austin Weekly newspaper "The Poet" of her west side community.

Today, Ms. Tanksley is a contributing writer for the Citizen Newspaper and a published author and actress. She describes herself as "a writer by inspiration and an actress by aptitude."

"**There Is An Oasis** is an artful, creative and vibrant manifestation of its author. This youthful, poetic, lyricist spills inspirational messages that uplift the spirit and define our multi-faceted culture. LaKisha's works will blossom and rise as sure as the sun does for years to come."

— **Paul Davis,** *Managing Editor Citizen Newspaper Chicago, Il.*

TABLE OF CONTENTS

Dedication
Acknowledgments
A Letter from the Author
Tribute to My Childhood
Introduction

Oasis	2
Wake Up!	3
Success	5
Black Pride	6
Why	7
A Friend	8
Test Your Memories	9
Crossed Road...	10
Dare	11
Memories	12
Visions	13
God Is.	15
All of Me	17
Reach	19
God's Design	21
The Value of a Mother	23
4 Dollars an Hour	24
Someone You	25
A Psalm of Hope	26
Make Haste	27
It's Left Up to Us	28
Doubts	29
The End	30
If I Could Fly	31
Listen More	31
Bend	32
Sorry	33
Black Flower	35
The Power of Prayer	36
Lord, Let Your Will Be Done	37
Genesis	38
Faults Within Thoughts	39
I Can't Live Without You	40
I Know God Will	41

Can?   42
Love Doesn't Hurt   43
Moon By Night   45
Is?   46
Just Wait   47
Forever   48
Grandma Said   49
Nothings New   51
Slavery   52
Why Me?   53
Golden Seal   54
I Swam 21 Hours   55
Made Out of Me   57
Beginning School   58
Grown Folks   59
Boys, Boys, Boys   60
Believe   60
Words Mean a World of a Lot   61
Bumble Bee   63
Discovery   64
The Night Your Lights Went Out   65
Shooting Star   66
Love Conquers   67
Prove To Me   68
Biggest Birthday Kiss   69
Ku Klux Klan   70
No   71
Life   73
Lion Hearted   75
Hello Jesus, Goodbye Cocaine!   76
Love And Time   78
No Greater Love   78
Put It in the Master's Hand   80
Love Song   81
Good Friends Are For Keeps   82
Fair Lady   83
Strong Love   84
Love's Revival   85
Love's Test   86
Mr. Taps   89
Woman   90
Wake Up And Become An Achiever   91

DEDICATION

I would like to dedicate this book in memory of the belated, Walter Lee Anderson, Jr. and to all the young men and women like him, who have died an unfortunate death as a result of gang and drug wars. Please, for the sake of our future, pass this book on to the youth, who are influenced by gangs and peer pressure, so that they can discover THERE IS AN OASIS, an exit to peace and hope through struggle.

Increase the peace, decrease the violence.

ACKNOWLEDGMENTS

Before all others, let me start by acknowledging my Lord and Creator of every good and perfect gift, Jesus Christ. Without the support and faith from God, I couldn't imagine being able to write one sentence. I know that the primary source of all my help comes from the Lord!

To my mother, Debra Louise Tanksley; my grandmothers, Anita Tanksley, Louise Bianca Tanksley, Bernice Smith, and Norma Reese; and grandfathers, William Tanksley and Offe Reese. To my younger sister, Nikki Nicole and my two brothers, Alfred and Kevian. To my entire family.

To all my friends, mentors and supporters; Kenny Coleman, George Jones, Joe Greenwood, Earnest Taylor, Annette Crosby, Mary Adair, Janis Parker, Christopher Lentz, Liliana Drechney, Kenny Mac, Pastor Aarron Holmes of New St. Mark Church, Carmen Vacquez, Kisia Fells, Marcel Jacobs and the entire Awakening Cast, Erie King III, Gerald T. Smith, William Kilgore, Edward Carter, Percy Billings, and Rev. Jerry L. Jones. Mentors: Maya Angelo, Gwendolyn Brooks, Oprah Winfrey, Les Brown, Jesse Jackson, Jawanza Kunjufu, Martin Luther King Jr., Shirley Ceasar, Michael Jordan, and Ben Vereen.

A LETTER FROM THE AUTHOR

Dear Readers:

Most young authors would begin the first page of their book by saying, "Hello, my name is Lakisha Marie Tanksley. I am 22 years old; my credits include being a poet, lyricist, playwright, and actress. Then the characters in their story grows up gracefully. How unrealistic! No struggle; no triumph; no fight; no glory."

My style of writing is a bit more realistic. I will not paint a deceitful picture that is peaceful and pretty, concealing the troubling issues which effect our communities. As for me, being considered a young, Black, talented writer, it would cramp my style by telling you something opposite of truth. Therefore, I will not do that. What you will find in this book are the realities of life, expressed in motivational poetry. This book provides an alternative to depression, drug addiction, low self-esteem, poverty or any other negative influences you may have. I am confident you will be inspired after reading this book. Then you will discover, there is an oasis. A perfect exit to peace and hope through struggle.

My deepest love,

Lakisha M. Tanksley

Lakisha M. Tanksley

P.S. Life and its circumstances may not always paint a pretty picture. That's quite alright because all it takes is one willing and able person to stand up and project positive change.

TRIBUTE TO MY CHILDHOOD

As a young child growing up in Chicago, I would always fantasize about becoming a well known poet. Maintaining this courageous vision as a youngster, wasn't easy. However, I was continually inspired by the faith and the rejuvenating ambition of my mother. In spite of tough times, she would never lose her smile. I envied the hope and peace she maintained with or without food for our family to eat.

Yes, I am an African-American female, who grew up in a low income family and a drug infested environment. This is not a complaint, just a fact. The greatest thing I have discovered in the memory of my past and journey toward my future is, I have found an oasis. Better known as, my exit to peace and hope through struggle. Discovering the same confidence and forti- tude my mother reveals in her smile, I began to express in my poetry. I conceived at the age of eight, becoming a well-known poet as my life's goal. Later at the age of thirteen, becoming a well-known author was adopted as my life's destiny. There is an oasis.

Introduction

Rhythm of Joy
(Motivational Poetry)

First, let me tell you something about motivational poetry. Motivational poetry is best described as rhythm of joy. Why would I describe motivational poetry as rhythm? R-H-Y-T-H-M (rhythm) is the movement of harmony, music or sound. You see, motivational poetry is just like rhythm. Motivation will move your spirit by encouragement and reminding you that you are somebody! That's why motivation is best described as the rhythm of joy.

THERE IS AN OASIS

A Collection of Motivational Poems by Lakisha Marie Tanksley

OASIS

The wind and waves lead me to a place where joy never dies.
To a path of certainty, better known as a peaceful paradise.
Far beyond the range of carnal vision into a realm of optimism.
To a secret place where love and hope remains.
A fortress where dreams and goals sustain.
Sheltering me in dreadful storms and tides.
An oasis of redemption is where joy and peace is revived.
There is an oasis.

WAKE UP!

Wake up, wake up,
before I shake you up.
You always arrive in late.
Wake up, wake up, it's morning time.
I say rise and shine, while there is still time.

If you seek success, you will find success.

SUCCESS

Success is the core of my existence.
The Manifestation will appear with time.
Determination is what my dreams are made of.
So when I seek I will find.
Find a glittering pot of willpower, deep within my soul.
When success, determination, inspiration, and willpower are tried in the fire,
They will come out as pure as gold.

BLACK PRIDE

I'm proud to be black this is a fact.
Our heritage is filled with strength and deter-
mination.
This pride centers around a well rounded edu-
cation.
While still being proud of who I am and what
I can do,
Others will notice change in my life too.
Friends and family can help this promise stay,
by letting their actions reflect their pride
today.

WHY?

Why let life's opportunities slip right down the drain?
Without determination, you'll always lose and never gain.
Do not underestimate your own capabilities, and say you can't win.
Because there is lots of strength and power deep within.
Deep within your mind and soul just look and see.
You've got more than what it takes to be the best in what you want to be.

A FRIEND

Is it possible to find a friend like you?
So impossible it seems, for this request to come true.
Is it possible to whisper without being spread abroad?
Yes it is possible when the conversation is with God.
Words from the wise; listen to many but speak to few.
It is impossible to find a friend like you.

TEST YOUR MEMORIES

Test your memories so you can see,
How bad or good you have treated me.
Test the memories of your soul.
This test will prove that you are bold.
Test the quality of your voice.
This test will prove I'm your best choice.
Test your memories if you could.
And now you love me like you should.

CROSSED ROAD...

The road may seem too hard to cross.
Seeing no light, your way seems lost.
Just keep on walking by faith and not by
sight.
Remember, with God on your side, everything
will be alright.

DARE

Dare to be different is my battle cry.
I can make it, is the tune I sigh.
Daring to be different is the song I sing.
Resisting peer pressure and every hindering
thing.
Removing every stumbling block out of my
way.
Waiting patiently in the night for the breaking
of the day.
While daring to be different on the road to
success.
Give it more than just a try, give it all you've
got.
Do your best.

MEMORIES

Memories of our struggle for freedom.
Memories of many wars in an unrighteous king-
dom.
Memories of worthless land burned to waste.
Memories of bondage toward the black race.
Memories of possible missions and impossible
tasks.
Memories of Doctor Martin Luther King, Jr.
who helped man believe freedom and justice
will last.

VISIONS

*I can see visions of a rising sunset taking place
in your life.
Visions of no more pain, sorrows or strife.
Visions of strength that lift you above any
obstacles that would come in your way.
Visions of freedom, joy, and laughter in my visions
of a brighter day.*

Whatever is lovely,
Whatever is pure,
Whatever is righteous
Whatever is true.
God is...

God Is.

If you're searching for love that won't cost you
a broken heart.
Just turn on the lights, having no communion
with dark.
God is a lamp unto your feet.
God is a path when there is no way.
God is love like no other, and everlasting love
that's here to stay.
If you need love, it's already here.
A love that is unfailing, God can wipe away
your tears.
If you want to purchase love, the price is
already paid.
A price paid in suffering that you might be
saved.
God can save you from sin's imitation love and
all of sin's attachments.
A package full of artificial cures and burden
fragments.
Bits and pieces of bondage like pain, drugs,
fear, sickness
and sin.
Imitation love has death, hell and destruction
as its end.
So, why not accept a love of value that is true.
God is the problem free love that's best for you.

Confidence and self-esteem is an element of beauty all by itself. So hold on to self-esteem inspite of personal dislikes and short-comings. Just take the good with the bad and don't get discouraged. Just get better. So as a man thinketh, so is he!

Stay encouraged; keep integrity, stay proud... Keep on smiling and remember, self-esteem is strength and willpower that can only be found and stored within one's self.

All Of Me

My blackness is beautiful, my shade so plentiful.
I love me by being me.
I correct myself when I make a mistake.
I have discovered many unique and important
character traits.
A trait of creativity, a trait of modesty.
A trait of friendliness, a trait of elegance.
A perfected creature in God's likeness.
A trait of honesty and politeness.
A trait of strong pride and strong will.
How great it is to be black.
How wonderful it feels.

There comes a challenging time in everyone's life when your goals seem too far to reach. Suddenly you become doubtful and afraid because it hurts too much to believe. What if it never happens? is one dreadful question puzzling your mind. With so much doubt and pressure for success, it may seem easier to give up. Please don't give up, and don't give in; remember, your goals are waiting on you. You'll always be successful if you believe in yourself and never, ever, compromise or give up!

REACH

Reach for the stars,
No matter how far.
Your dreams may seem too far from here.
But as you reach, your dreams come near.
So move forward and pursue.
You've got the power to make your dreams come
true.
Just move your faith on up a little higher.
Knowing you can win.
Knowing you will triumph, reach for the stars,
No matter how far.
Acknowledging God in all you do.
With the help of God, your dreams can come
true.

If you currently live in the same drug infested environment that I grew up in, I know from experience that it's not easy looking outside your window and having a desire to smile...because your neighborhood is nothing like what you see on the Cosby Show. Instead of basketball courts, gift shops and ice cream parlors for recreation, we have drug dealers, prostitution and liquor stores on every corner. Is this a reason to hold your head down and give up hope? No! So what, life and its circumstances aren't always good to you. That doesn't mean you should stop being good to yourself . Now you can hold your head up high and stop all that unnecessary crying. You take some tissue child and wipe your tears, blow your nose and just remember...Life is what you make it! It ain't over till it's over! So don't cry, just make your life better!

P.S. You have the choice in life to fight or get your butt kicked.

God's Design

Black boy, black girl, lift up your bowed down head.
Black boy, black girl wipe the tears from your eyes that shed.
Black boy, black girl, do you know who you are?
Do you know where you come from?
You are an African-American jewel with family descendants from Africa.
Black boy, black girl do you have a dream?
Black child, where is your integrity, determination or self-esteem?
Black boy, black girl do you believe in yourself? Do you have pride?
Lift up your heads, black boy, black girl, you are important and unique.
You are one of God's precious designs!

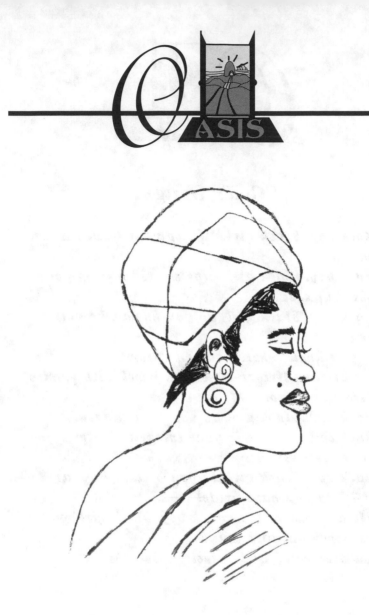

The value of a loving mother is priceless. It is indeed an honor to share and receive love from a loving mother. Remember to let motherly love continue.

The Value of a Mother

There are many things of value found in this
world today.
For example, the importance of rain for the
flowers.
The importance of sunlight for day.
There are so many things of value, like dia-
monds,
pearls and gold.
But the love and value of a mother, never could
be sold.
I love you mom, more than you could ever
imagine, much more than words can express.
If I were offered one million dollars to replace
your love,
I know I would refuse the offer because mom,
you're the best.

4 DOLLARS AN HOUR

Did you say you'd like to pay me four dollars an hour?
Let the poor stay weak, let the rich keep the power.
Are you telling me, one minute of my time isn't even worth a dime?
Man, I don't think you're right, take a hike.
Four dollars isn't enough for me to buy a descent pair of underwear!
So, I know it's not worth my time
Only, one hundred pennies, four quarters, twenty nickels and ten dimes, not!
You know I have experience, and I'm the best one for the job.
I have three years experience in customer relations, I work very hard.
Four dollars an hour!
I have better things to do with my time, than to be your peanut salary slave.
I can find a much better job somewhere else and get paid.
I know because I need a job and I'm a so-called minority, me not excepting your offer kind of shook yah.
But listen up, I'm no fool, I do know that self-preservation is the first law of nature.
Oh yeah, self don't like to be used, confused and abused.
Four dollars an hour is confusing to me.
Just take your job with no paying salary and ship it up your butt.
Let me say goodbye, and don't wish me none of your good luck.

SOMEONE YOU

Where is that someone, who can make a difference?
Oh where could this someone be?
Where is that someone who can run the distance,
far beyond eyes could see?
Oh where is this someone? Oh why delay?
Where is hope? Oh where I pray?
Where is this someone who will take a stand.
Is there one willing vessel, heart soul, or man?
I never promised making a difference would be
a smooth sail, so get ready to fight.
Keep your vision in focus, never give up, never
loose sight.
Discouragement will come with doubts and
fears.
This change may cost you hard times and tears.
But after the rain the sun always shines
through.
There is someone who can make a difference,
and that someone is you.

A PSALM OF HOPE

Yea, though I walk and experience many
troubles.
Trouble won't last always.
The sky may be cloudy, but the sun will shine
one day.
Oh, one day I will smell fresh flowers then smile
with great joy,
As I listen to birds sing and the laughter of
young girls and boys.
So much beauty in the earth, one day I will see,
While gazing at the sky, birds, land and trees;
The flowers, rainbows, stars and moon.
Oh, there will be a brighter day soon and very
soon.

MAKE HASTE

Make haste oh God to deliver me.
Send your peace to calm the sea.
Make haste oh Lord, and help me stand.
Send help God, stretch out your hand.
Oh Lord there is violence in the wind.
Free me from bondage, I'm captured by sin.
Make haste oh God, your name I call.
Make haste oh Lord, don't let me fall.
Make haste oh God, deliver me.
Make haste oh Lord, and set me free.

IT'S LEFT UP TO US

It's left up to us...
Christopher Columbus discovered America, the
land of the brave and free.
It's left up to us...
Martin Luther King Jr., had a dream for all
men to live in equality.
It's left up to us...
Abraham Lincoln in American history, January
1, 1863, wrote the Emancipation Proclamation.
It's left up to us...
Martin had a dream, you have a dream, I have
a dream.
It's left up to us...

DOUBTS

Doubt the sun as if there's no sky.
Doubt the harmony in most lullabies.
Doubt the day that's appointed for man to die.
Doubt your sorrow as you cry.
Doubt burning candles on the birthday cake.
Doubt that glass is solid and it can break.
Doubt fire burns.
Doubt birds fly.
Doubts can hinder your progress, but time still goes by.

THE END

If you mingle with matches, you'll soon get burnt.
If you mess with owned property, you'll soon get hurt.
Tell me the purpose of this thing.
If you tamper with a scorpion, just be prepared for its sting.
One thing leads to another and then some more.
So just release all the tension and let me go.
We well know this is not right; I'm not yours and you're not mine.
Just like peaches aren't roses and water's not wine.
So lets pull down the curtain and end the show.
Now lets exit from the hearts and let it go.

IF I COULD FLY

If I could fly, I would fly to the highest point
of the sky.
Then I could see the heavens prepared for me.
With my golden wings, I would fly, fly, fly; if
I could fly.

LISTEN MORE

Man is born with two ears and one mouth;
this means we must listen more.

BEND

In order not to break, you sometimes bend.
Some bend from pressure, some from love.
Many from troubles, some none of the above.
Circumstances may cause you to bend;
But don't you break.

SORRY

Sorry that I wasted time.
Feeling like an unused dime.
Sitting in a dark and lonely pocket.
Right about now, my determination plug has
lost its socket.
My hopes and dreams are shattering;
this feeling of defeat so damaging.
I've tried and tried to escape.
But lots of strength it'll have to take;
for me to throw past misfortune away and
begin a brand new start today.

The color black is so wonderful! Being black is
beautiful, and the shades of black so lovely. You
know, I can appreciate the positive connotation of
a black berry. When searching for the sweetest
fruit you never look for a light, unripe, sour
berry. But the darker berries are most popular
for their sweetness. It's time for us as African-
American people to have pride and appreciate our
heritage and stop looking at each other saying,
"Uhhhn! She so black!" But instead say, "Ooh!
She so sweet!" The darker the fruit, the sweeter
the juice.

BLACK FLOWER

A little black flower, planted with a seed of
grace.
The expression of joy shines on it's face.
A little black flower, so beautifully divine.
An elegant structure in this flower you will
find.
Love and the joys of happiness, this shows a
black flower's elegance.
The colors of this flower so proudly stand out.
You are a little black flower, without a doubt.

THE POWER OF PRAYER

You prayed all day and night.
While the problem seemed unable to turn out right.
Satan came and told you, never, no way.
But God's Holy Spirit reminds you to always pray.
Remember, faith cometh by hearing and believing God's word.
The first day you prayed, an answer was sent, and your prayer was heard.

LORD, LET YOUR WILL BE DONE

Lord let your will be done in my life today.
Search me Master and wash my sins away.
Lord, I am willing to accept you as the leader
of my life.
Remove all pains, misery and strife.
Lord let your spirit wash me through and
through.
Rebuild my life, make me brand new.

GENESIS

The day begins, as your dreams unfold.
So far from home but near your goals.
The sun is still shining, the birds still sing.
How beautiful, how marvelous, is the joy the
day brings.
Look at this great big world;
What a magnificent piece of art.
Today is the beginning of a new day;
and right where you stand, your dream now
starts.

FAULTS WITHIN THOUGHTS

Strife and grief with tormenting thoughts,
Dwelling within man's unreasonable faults.
Thoughts that dwell in human ways.
Faults that darken sunny days.
With damaging feelings causing strife and
grief.
At the drop of a hat, here comes that old thief.
He stole someone else's love and threw it away.
And replaced it with faults within thoughts in
their hearts to stay.

I CAN'T LIVE WITHOUT YOU

I can live without birds singing.
I can live without autumn leaves.
I can live without winter snow flakes.
I can live without the summer and spring.
I can exist without money.
I can picture a world without stars.
I can survive without a man.
I can reside without a fancy car.
I would enjoy life without musical horns.
I can continue without many things in life
But I can't live without the Lord.

I KNOW GOD WILL

I reckon that the suffering of this present time can not be compared to the glory that will be revealed in us.
For the Lord is my light and my salvation, in Him I put my trust.
God is my redeemer, He will deliver me.
Just like He delivered the Israelites when he divided the Red Sea.
I'm waiting on the Lord, I know He will deliver.

CAN?

Can you see the sadness of my tears?
Can you sense the torment of my fears?
Can you see the confusion of my walk?
Can you hear the curiosity in my talk?
Can you feel a chill from my frozen heart?
All these feelings just pull me apart.
Pulling my heart of love here and there.
Sadness, torment, fear, confusion, and curiosity,
with the chill from life's struggle is everywhere.

LOVE DOESN'T HURT

The initials of love aren't the design of this
bruise.
The colors of love, are not black, purple and blue.
The expressions of love aren't the sad song I sigh.
The melody of love isn't in my cry.
The feelings of love are not expressed in pain.
Child abuse and love are not the same.

The moon is the heavenly body next to the earth, poetically described as the brother of the earth.

MOON BY NIGHT

The moon by night is the prettiest sight.
The moon shows an elegant gleam;
Sort of blue and white such a beautiful thing.
The moon shines so bright at night, because Mr.
Moon is saying "good night."

IS?

Is pure, pure?
Is sweet, sweet?
Is tare, tare?
Is wheat, wheat?
Is love, love?
Is lust, lust?
Is God, Good?
Is trust, trust?
Is divine from heaven and sent from God?
Pure is pure.
Sweet is sweet.
Tare is tare.
Wheat is wheat.
Love is love.
Lust is lust.
God is good.
In Him I trust.

JUST WAIT

If you wait until you're grown,
and stop doing everything wrong.
Just wait, maybe then you'll see, how great
your future can really be.
If you and I just wait, we will make it
through life's successful highway gate.
Then you and I can discover a virtue of
patience, that will make our successful dreams
a reality.
Just wait.

FOREVER

My God is forever giving me words to say.
Encouraging words of wisdom inspiring me each
day.
Great joy remains now and forever.
In God I put my trust and build my endeavors.

GRANDMA SAID

When life's struggle gets too hard
and you think about giving in.
If you can't see hope for a brighter future and
it looks like you can't win.
Child, then close your eyes and remember words
of wisdom, Grandma said.
Wear wisdom's garment on your body; and
crown wisdom's ornament on your head.
Grandma's words were, "never give up, just hold
on; times will get better, it won't be long.
The wind must blow and rain must fall.
No pain, no gain, no battle, no triumph.
Winning is never easy, but child, you never give
up!"

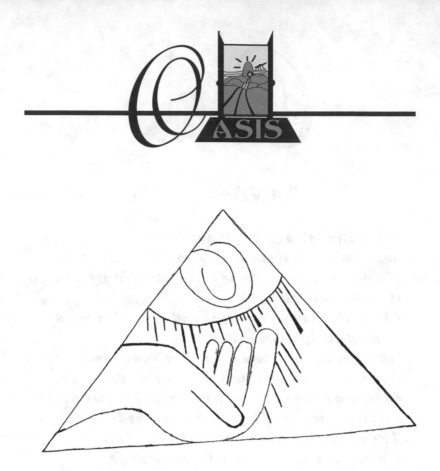

There's nothing new under the sun is an old popular saying that we all can attest to. Life is a circle, it goes round and round and round.

NOTHING'S NEW

I once knew what you now know...
I've put on the same glamorous, obscene show.
I once saw what you now see.
And I've heard what you now hear.
I've loved with the same old love.
And hated with the same old hate.
I've been bored, and I've also had my share of
fun.
But child, this one thing you should know;
There is nothing new under the sun.

SLAVERY

Once there were bare fields and a segregated civilization, with repeated acts of discrimination.
Justice hid and no justice found.
Millions of African families tormented and bound.
The words of an African-American who once feared these dangers.
Only the truth can heal our wounded angers.

WHY ME?

Why do you choose to pick on me?
Do I look like a southern apple tree?
Picking from me because of greed; that's not
fair.
Leaving my branches lonely and my appearance
bare.
Do you like my shinny color; do you think I'm
cute?
Infatuation can be aggravating and that's what
you do.

GOLDEN SEAL

Under the river and over the sea,
Me and my sparkling coat that gleams.
I splash and dance and prance and kick.
I live in the sea and I move very quick.
I am the golden seal you see; isn't my skin so
lovely on me?
Because I'm the pride beneath the sea, this is
what makes me lovely you see.

I SWAM 21 HOURS

I swam for 21 hours in a very large sea.
Hoping and praying for help to come rescue me.
I began to panic, swiftly seeing no signs of rescue near.
Overwhelmed by this situation, submerged in fear.
Time is moving too fast and my life is passing by.
I wish I had the strength of an eagle and its mighty wings so that I could fly high above this great sea of horror and find a peaceful paradise to stay.
I swam 21 hours in a day, as I reached land, determination came my way.

Love is indeed a necessity among family and friends. My mother, two brothers, little sister and I have lots of love for each other. Dad doesn't live with us but, I'm sure if he'd visit sometime, he would express love to us as well. Yes, I grew up in a single family home unlike my friends at school. I felt kind of strange not having a dad around. Now that I'm older I understand, that it didn't make me strange at all because it wasn't my fault. My mother, two brothers, little sister and I are still one happy family because we appreciate one another. I like my sister a lot, even when she throws my clothes out the window when no one's watching; and tries to follow me everywhere I go. My sister is bad sometimes, but that doesn't stop me from loving her. You know, everyone says she's cute, but they don't realize it's because she looks just like me.

MADE OUT OF ME

The pesky things that my little sister may say.
She learned from me the other day.
The unwanted tears that I once cried are the
same old tears she hold inside.
The annoying laugh that I might do.
I caught her doing that same laugh too.
The songs I sing, the words I say;
She learns these things from me everyday.
Made out of me, as you can see; the things we
enjoy are the same.
In my little sister's book, I'm her fame.
Every little thing my little sister may do.
I just remembered, I did them too.

BEGINNING SCHOOL

First I greet you with a frown, as you look me up and down.
Then I roll my eyes at you, then watch your face turn pale and blue.
Walking pass stumping my feet, thinking what a terrible person to meet.
Speaking to you with a cry and a shout, with no remark but one big pout.
Why did this brat have to come to me, this is the most unpleasant kindergarten you could ever see.

GROWN FOLKS

Most grown folks argue and hear me not.
Sometimes I wish they would just stop.
Just stop picking always on me.
I have a lot of wisdom; they're too old to see.
They don't understand my emotions, as tears
flow down my face.
I wish they'd stop trying; I don't know how
much more I can take.
Mom, I do know when I'm wrong; Dad, I do
know when I'm right.
Oh please Lord, show them the light.
Grown folks?

BOYS, BOYS, BOYS

Boys can be good; boys can be bad, some glad
and some sad.
They come big or small; they come skinny or fat
or even black or white.
But I know one thing; their all dynamite.

BELIEVE

"Can not" is not true!
All things are possible if you just believe.

WORDS MEAN A WORLD OF A LOT

Words mean a world of a lot.
Words can move you like the wind.
Words can communicate as bright as the sun.
Words can express personality in people.
Words uncover hidden character traits.
Words can build strong nations, and words can
cause destruction.
Words can wound hearts.
Words can heal the body and soul.
Words are very powerful.
Words can embrace you with joy.
Words can drown you in tears.
Words mean a world of a lot.
So be very careful with the words you use.

Bumble bees have a song of their own.
Bzzzzz!

BUMBLE BEE

*A bumble bee is yellow and black, the prettiest
colors.
A bumble bee hums so beautifully.
As it flies, it sings and dances in honey
romance.*

DISCOVERY

If I freely may discover how to please my lov-
ing mother.
I'd be willing to become more fair and witty.
Working harder at home and city.
Building goals which never will destroy.
Words that are sweet makes her enjoy.
Not so easy nor very harsh.
All extremes to please mom, I'll take part.

THE NIGHT YOUR LIGHTS WENT OUT

The night your lights went out.
I paced my mind with doubt.
I've lost someone I dearly love.
A lost love highly ranked above.
A love that journeyed too far for man to find.
Love buried beneath soil yet found in my mind.
The thought of death hurts, while tears glide
down my cheeks.
My heart is over boiling, I feel sorrows heat.
When rain drops fall on my window pane.
My tears of sadness drowns them away.
How can I find strength to dispose these feel-
ings of sorrow today?
Only by depending on God to make a brighter
day.

SHOOTING STAR

If I had one wish that would come true.
I'd wish my life was perfect and my outer
appearance brand new.
How about a bright and shinny look, like dia-
monds and gold?
What would life be like to be a shooting star?
Do stars grow old?
Five glittering head ornaments and a home up
so high.
Gliding across the heavens and space up in the
sky.
I wish I was a shooting star, a descendant of
the sun.
God would be my neighbor and the angels up
above.

LOVE CONQUERS

My heart warmly welcomes your love near.
Love will attract many obstacles but, true love
will conquer fear.
My mind openly receives every challenge true
love will cost.
It's a privilege to give true love a try; it's a
chore when the love is lost.
My eyes willingly uncover the book of promises
that I read in your eyes.
My memory redeems joy and laughter even as I
cry.
My spirit discerns devotion and truth in every
single kiss.
My love for you is included in every dream
and every wish.
My nature communicates in passion when you
hold me near.
My heart once again welcomes you and love
will conquer all my fears.

PROVE TO ME

Prove to me that you love me.
Prove to me that you'll never hurt me.
After this you can discontinue the search for
me.
Prove to me you'll never go away.
Prove to me true love is here to stay.
Prove to me your love is real.
Prove to me it's still a thrill.
Prove to me I'm your number one.
Prove to me I'm the only one.
Prove to me and say I do.
This will prove your love is true.

BIGGEST BIRTHDAY KISS

My birthday is coming and don't you know?
I'd love a giant ice cream cone.
But if that's just too hard to find,
I'd love a phone to save a dime.
But all I got was a giant kiss;
and a face full of red sticky lip stick.

P.S. Mother's biggest birthday kiss.

KU KLUX KLAN

July 6, 1995

Mr. Black Boy
P.O. Box Sellout
Slavery County 66600

Dear Mr. Black Boy,

Hello, you want to be my slave and join the Ku Klux Klan. Don't you want to kill your brother, drug deal, and gang bang? No need for you to ride a horse and wear a white cutup sheet. All you do is sell your soul and a little dope for me. Go contaminate your home and streets, but don't you visit mine. Shut up, listen, and follow orders, nigga serve your time. So come on, be my puppet, sucker and my fool. No need to have any morals man; just be cool, gang bang, drug deal, and act just like a KKK. Black boy, you enjoy killin' up your brothers; now that's a low down dirty shame.

For Real, Ku Klux Klan
P.O. Box Gotcha
Heartless County 66600

NO

*I know you didn't just ask me, "Would I like to sell
dope?"*
*Do I look like Mr. Tom the sellout? You must think
my life's a joke.*
*Well listen up, ha, ha, ha. My pockets may be
empty, and my livin' arrangements are kind of bad.*
*But killin' up your own is even worst. Sellin' poison
to your community is sad.*
*Wake up man; look all around you and see all the
damaging things drugs have done.*
*Taking the lives of innocent children; destroying fami-
lies one by one.*
*I ain't crazy, I know all about the drug business and
what it can offer both you and me.*
*Twenty years or more in a penitentiary, a luxurious
coffin, custom made.*
Eternity in hell is what it guarantees.
*Push on, don't come tellin' me about profit in a busi-
ness that hires me to sell out.*
Man, you think you sellin' drugs to make a livin'.
But you sellin' your future with no doubt.
*I can clearly remember how the violence of drugs
stole and broke my family apart.*
*Man, it rushed in and shook us up like an earth-
quake.*
Then bang, shot my oldest brother in the heart.
*Yeah, all drugs can do for me is kill my oldest broth-
er and leave me and my mama here to cry.*
Just stop the madness. My answer is no! So goodbye.

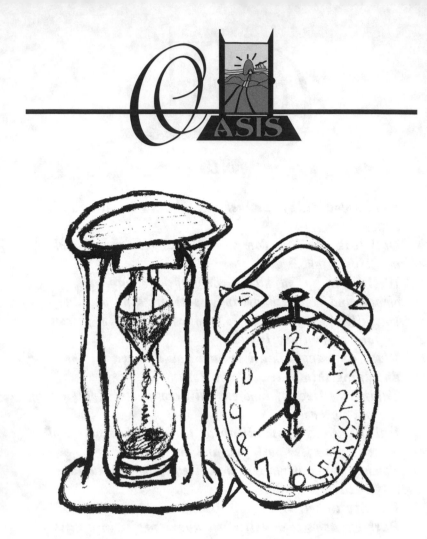

Life is too short to be taken for granted.

LIFE

Life is filled with transitions.
Young becomes old.
Rainbows disappear.
Self-esteem can be discouraged
Courage can become fear.
Happy faces and joyful hearts, can sometimes
be sad.
Sunny days with frustrations, can cause a per-
fectly good day to go bad.
Seconds change into minutes.
Minutes change into hours.
A seed planted in soil with proper
rain and sunlight, can grow into a lovely
flower.
Friendships may grow distant because of prob-
lems and pain.
Times are filled with transitions, but I love
you just the same.

With the heart of a lion, you can attack the negative statistics and prove them all to be wrong. By lifting up your eyes to a higher realm of optimism that will and can give you the strength and courage to accomplish your life goals. Dreams become reality when you believe and take actions concerning them.

LION HEARTED

Don't you tell me that I can not win!
Oh, yes I can!
Don't come tellin' me that I will fall!
Because I can stand!
Don't you lie and say it's impossible!
It's possible, I do believe.
I know what I want. I know what I need.
Don't you tell me about the winning odds; you
can not change my mind.
If I don't come out triumphant, at least I'm
brave.
Because I tried.

Reach out to Jesus.

Hello Jesus, Goodbye Cocaine!

What has happened to your dreams?
Where is determination? Where is your self-esteem?
You once ranked your goals in life so high.
Not always succeeding, but at least you tried.
You once tried to fulfill your life's goals.
But now you sit content as your life is sold.
Sold for a packaged deal named cocaine.
Full of suicidal problems and pains. *(cont.)*

Aren't you tired of cocaine's monkey on your back?
Such a heavy load with a burden sack.
Cocaine is filled with hate and you need love.
Right now you need comfort, and cocaine gives you a shove.
As you sniff and as you smoke, your life is being destroyed by this thing called coke.
Your hopes and integrity begin to shed.
Your soul is lost and your brain almost dead.
Shedding away one by one,
No family, no love, no future, no one.
Remember you sold your life for a fifteen minute thrill.
Did you enjoy your trips to wonderland with sights unreal?
A trip destroying many families, so many dreams, so many goals, for cocaine don't let your life be sold.
Wait, don't give up, let me introduce you to a friend.
To fulfill your life's emptiness, Jesus I recommend.
Hello Jesus; goodbye cocaine.
Hello sunshine; goodbye rain.
Hello peace; goodbye sorrows.
Hello hope for tomorrow.
The Lord can pick up your life's broken pieces and give you the strength to stand.
Giving you freedom in place of bondage;
I know that God can.
God can knock cocaine's monkey off your back.
Restoring your fortitude by putting your life on the right track.

LOVE AND TIME

Love and time are endless.
Love continues, and time keeps on going.
Love and time grows.
Passion grows when love increases,
and knowledge expands with time.
Time and love are costly.
Time's price is patience.
Love's price is endurance.
Love and time are eternal.
Time is forever reoccurring.
Love goes on and on, and on.
Time and love are everlasting.
Our friendship never dies.
Each moment I think of you,
love and time are revived.

NO GREATER LOVE

<u>Friend:</u> *I've moped around feeling misery for much*
too long!
feeling grieved and depressed singing my sad
song.
Every day to me seems dark and my troubles
remain. Girlfriend , I know what I need is love,
to drive away the pain!
Instead of looking up I desire to hold my head
down.

*behind my confused emotions is a lonely heart of
disgust and a pretty face with a frown.
Upset with this world, but excepting it's curse.
wanting to express my feelings, but I'm afraid
of the results of the outburst.
I'm tired of life's chaos!
I'm searching for peace!
I'm tired of stress and troubles!
I'm yearning for relief!
Sweet relief from pain and sorrows, lookin' for
a strong man to bare; all my weights and troubles.
Is there any one who cares?
Girl, you said you knew a man who would wipe
away my tears. You said he'd rescue me in times
of trouble, no need to fear!
You told me he was rich!
But, will he supply my every need?
Witness: He'll be your man, money and lover, he
wants to be your every thing!
Friend: Girlfriend what is his name?
Just look what you have done!
Witness: Some call him the lilly of the valley and
the bright and mornin' sun.
Friend: I'll call him Mr. super man lover then give
him my whole heart. Tell me, when can I meet him?
When will this rendezvous start?
Tell me now don't leave out a clue!
Witness: Ok, There is no greater love!
Friend Gods love is unfailing, his love is best for
you!*

PUT IT IN THE MASTER'S HAND

Darkness may overshadow the peace in your life.
Trouble will increase with envy and strife.
Trials may last a little bit longer.
Stubborn obstacles may stand a little bit stronger.
But be strong and have faith that you can stand.
Life is so much better when you put everything in the Master's hands.

LOVE SONG!

*Jesus is the best thing that could ever happen
to me.
Just as the hart panteth after the water brooks,
so panteth my soul after thee.
Because he introduced me to peace when there
was corruption in my life.
He's eliminated from my heart doubt, fear and
strife.
By breaking up the sterile ground and replenish-
ing me with charity and righteousness.
The Lord has granted me with mercy and loving
kindness.
My first love is Jesus,
His name brings music to my ears, Sounding
like a soothing chant that drives away my tears.*

GOOD FRIENDS ARE FOR KEEPS

A brand new dawning
Gives me a Chance to say;
How the Lord will affect me
On this glorious day.

I can see God, Bringing joy
Out of old preserved rain;
I can see God shielding me
From my fears, and taking
Away my pain.

With a gracious and protective hand my Lord,
You guide me;
Through hail, rain, sleet and snow
You stick right beside me.

Being my post to lean on
When I begin to stumble;
I will hold on to my faith
And continue to be humble.

No one can compare,
Or even come close;
You're the first on my list,
And you're the best choice.

I choose to send you love,
Heart felt and sincere;
In hopes that your perfect friendship,
Continues through out this new dawning year.

FAIR LADY

Is the essence of my beauty a threat
Stalking and hunting me like a mink,
Luring me to fall in it's net?
Is the nature of my beauty my foe.
The sparkle in my eyes,
Form of my nose.
The softness of my skin,
Groove of my hips.
The contrast of my color,
And the curve of my hips.
Like a body of troops with rifles men aim my
way, In the peak of the morning and the closing
of the day.
Like birds early rising and stars late at night.
Many desire my love and for its possession they
will fight.

STRONG LOVE

Love is something we all could share.
Love is something everyone will declare.
If you love someone tell them so.
But don't forget to let love show.
Love is an old thing we show each day.
Don't forget, nothing can take strong love away,
Love is in the morning air.
Love can take you anywhere.
Love is a source no man can fight.
Love is a jewel we all should hold tight.
Love is in me and should be in you.
Love is special, love is kind.
If you show love, then plenty you will soon
find.

LOVE'S REVIVAL

A precious thought in the mind,
A precious thought so sweet and kind.
A precious thought that lives in your dreams.
A precious song that love sings.
A precious statement so highly ranked.
A long, long time it had to take,
For me to remove all bad thoughts away;
And live and love again today.

LOVE'S TEST

1. Is love a charming fellow tall dark and fine?
2. Is love in the colors of the rainbow or the taste of sparkling wine?

3. Is love the music or harmony songs bring?
4. Is love wedding bells or just a diamond ring?

5. Is love like compassion or a deep sense of care?
6. Is love being infatuated or just a longing to be there?

7. Is love like a puzzle you have to mix and match?
8. Is love like a turtle it's shelter is attached?

9. Is love like old age or teen age years?
10. Is love like courage over coming doubts and fears?

11. Is love unsolved that you conclude?
12. Is love like a postage stamp to stick it must be glued?

13. Is love like instant oatmeal just add water?
14. Is love a divider is love like a border?

15. Is love like a game you play by it's rules?
16. Is love an unsolved mystery small hints, large clues?

17. Is love like a tear of concern gliding down my face?
18. Is love an ethnic back ground color creed or race?

19. Is love just a season that melts away like snow?
20. Is love the autumns breeze as the wind may blow?

(cont.)

21. Is love the size of a mountain or the temperature of the sea?
22. Is love as strong as a lion and rooted like a tree?

23. Is love like a recipe that has to be made?
24. Is love like chloride bleach on color it may fade?

25. Is love everlasting can love just fade away?
26. Is love gone like the wind and as unexpected as the day?

27. Is love like my shadow it's there even when I hide?
28. Is love tall and skinny, is love fat and wide?

29. Is love quiet and timid or is love loud and bold?
30. Is love like heaven a prepared place for the righteous souls.

31. Is love like an aspirin it relieves the pain?
32. Is love important as the sunlight and much needed as the rain?

33. Is love like Lebanon filled with violence and death?
34. Is love like America filled with power and wealth?

35. Is love like hell fire and tears?
36. Is love like age measured by years?

37. Is love like a sport you play to win?
38. Is love like an investment you get out what you put in?

39. Is love just a flower with an everlasting scent?
40. Love is an undying emotion only momentarily spent.

*Tap dancing has a motivational message that
travels through rhythmic sounds.*

MR. TAPS

Where is the man with dancin' feet?
What is his name, oh where could he be?
Who is the man with rhythmic soul?
Can anybody tell me, does anybody know?
I said, I'm looking for a man with tap-to-the-
tap-tap groove.
When the music starts to play, his feet begins
to move.
Those beats, the rhythm and drums from the
mother land.
Oh where is the man with dancin' feet?
It won't hurt just to stand.
Again, I'm looking for a man with dancin' feet.
I wonder is he out there somewhere.
No, you are standing right behind me.
Mr. Taps!
You're the man with dancin' feet!
Could you do me a favor?
Would you dance for me?

WOMAN

You are the needle in the hay stack, and I am the thread.
WO + MAN = Woman.
The completeness of love to my heart you bring.
You're the man of my life and the star of my dreams.
You, the needle in a haystack, can I come in?
There is space in your heart for love to begin.
You, the needle in the haystack, I see you over there.
I want you closer, I'm calling you near.
You can't hide; I'm thread, I can see.
I have good taste; I choose the best quality.
Let us sew together and love complete.
I am like rain and you're the seed.
Let us grow together and enjoy this love.
Our love is divine and sent from above.

Wake Up And Become An Achiever

Once upon a time, there lived a young boy named Joe. Joe lived his entire life dreaming about becoming a professional basketball player just like Michael Jordan. Michael Jordan was his biggest idol. Although he couldn't afford to buy tickets to see the Chicago Bulls live at the stadium, he still enjoyed his front row seat in his bedroom. Viewing his 19 inch color television through his binoculars, as if he were at the stadium, he watched his godfather figure M. Jordan, fly to the basket with the greatest of ease and slam dunk the ball while all his fans cheered him on with amazement.

Watching video taped recordings of Michael Jordan was no new thing to Joe. That was his everyday routine; then he would put on his lucky jersey, the red t-shirt with the sleeves cut out and the number 23 written with a black marker on the front and back. He also wore red shorts to match.

Joe did a lot of pretending throughout his life. This young man believed that looking like Michael Jordan would some how help train him to play professional basketball. He was indeed a good sport and a loyal athlete. All he did was play ball.

However, he never took the time to learn how to become a professional ball player. He felt no need to ask questions to any of his basketball coaches or teachers about a scholarship. Day in and day out, all he did was play ball.

Joe's dream was to become an NBA star. How is this dream going to happen? Joe never asked this question. He was convinced that there was no need for professional training. He believed that he could advise and train himself. You see, he was better known as M.V.P. (most valuable player) on the basketball court in his neighborhood. So, Joe was convinced that all he had need of on the basketball court was his basketball and his homemade Jersey.

Oh boy, was this boy dreaming. How and when will his dreams be fulfilled? He played ball every Saturday because he had premonitions that one lucky day, success would come to him; while playing ball in the gym, some famous basketball coach would drive through his neighborhood and happen to stop at the gym. The coach then would single him out, noticing his great basketball talent and skillful moves. Suddenly, this famous basketball coach would draft him in the NBA. This was Joe's dream. And guess what? It was just a dream.

Sorry Joe, and a lot of us are just dreamers. Yes, we believe in ourselves just like Joe, but we fail to take actions. Hope without action is only a figment of one's imagination. Unfortunately, Joe's dream never became a reality. That doesn't mean dreams never come true. Again, it just means that hope without action is only a figment of one's imagination.

As we all may already know, every successful invention started off in the minds of the inventors as a dream, a vision, or a new idea. But, such great inventing pioneers, like George Washington Carver, Lewis Latimer, Charles Drew, Granville T. Woods and many more did not end their dreams with a mere conception. These great achievers took action; never accepting failure as an option and therefore designed a blueprint for success.

The important message behind this story is:

A dreamer is just a person
with high hopes for change.
But an achiever is one who
makes change happen.
Success never knocks on your door.
If you want success, you've
got to go for it, seek it,
research it, plan to achieve it,
then attain it.
Wake up!
And become an achiever!

Upon request, the owner of this book may receive
an autographed poetry message card of your choice
Size 3" x 5"
Cost $7.50 ea. plus $2.50 shipping and handling.

*Bonus gift with purchase of message card

Address your request and correspondence to
P.O. Box 20544
Chicago, IL 60620-0544

Please remember
1. Make check payable to Ms. Lakisha Tanksley
2. Include title and page number of poem.
3. Sign your check (Do not send cash)